LIVING

the

Rich

LIFE

SYLVESTER L. COSTON

ISBN 978-1-63903-677-6 (paperback)
ISBN 978-1-63903-678-3 (digital)

Christian Faith Publishing, Inc.
832 Park Avenue
Meadville, PA 16335
www.christianfaithpublishing.com

Printed in the United States of America

Chapter 1

THE JOURNEY

As I began the journey of living a rich life and rendering a great service to this great nation, I asked myself, *Are you ready?* The answer is, I would never think I'm ready. How could a young Black man born and raised in Central Park Village (which is a housing project in Tampa, Florida) to a teenage single mother and a father who disclaimed him ever feel ready for such a monumental task? For as long as I could remember, my family has always been poor—with poor education, poor health, and poor decision-making, coupled with poor values. I'd like to believe we were in this dire state of existence because of slavery and systemic oppression, but that would be me accepting a victim's mentality.

Truth is, we were poor because most accepted being poor and did little to change the circumstances. In fact, I'm convinced that most people not only accepted poverty but made poverty seem cool and created a culture that would keep someone poor—a culture steeped in child abandonment, pain, drugs, and ignorance and too invested in material things. However, it is true that slavery once broke Black families up, left unfit food for them to eat, and tortured, humiliated, killed, and subjected them to unpaid forced labor.

Times have changed living in the twenty-first century, I believe. We are living in an era where we have the opportunity to right most of those wrongs. Early on, my mission was not only to be a soldier in this great American battle against oppression, poverty, and lack of any kind for me and my family but to serve as an example for future generations to know that we will make it to that promised land Moses and Dr. King envisioned.

According to the dictionary, *rich* means "abundantly supplied with resources, means, or funds." The Bible provides an abundance of resources and served as a manual for my rich life.

Chapter 2

TRIBULATIONS AND TRIALS

It was during my time in high school that I decided to join the military after graduation. The thought came to me after I enjoyed a year in JROTC during my junior year. Not only did I know I had what it takes to be a good soldier, but I actually enjoyed learning and working in the program. But when I received an acceptance letter from the University of South Florida, my plans changed. I decided to embark on college and experience the college life, and any thoughts of the military were put far behind me. Honestly, I had no real plans for college, no idea what major I would concentrate on, or no real long-term vision. All I knew was I had an opportunity to pave a way and show my younger siblings and peers alike that it was possible to come from the projects and still go to college to make something out of yourself.

While on campus, I struggled, and I found it hard to connect with anyone. I was just another kid from the block taking advantage of an opportunity, but it seemed everyone else was on a mission. I would go to class, do the work, and excel with honors; but I still felt out of place and lacked any real direction. After changing majors at least three times, I decided to leave college and go back to the hood.

But when I went back, I found it wasn't the same as before; the project I knew was gone, and we were no longer kids hanging out and chasing small changes, but we were young men doing illegal grown-man business. Still, against my better judgment, I found myself in the thick of it—smoking drugs with guys I wouldn't trust to wash the inside of my car, buying and selling small bags of drugs, and kicking in my mother's door—and eventually found myself sleeping on the streets.

All this came to an abrupt halt on the evening I went to jail. That night I had been gambling, playing dice with the fellas on Ms. Tasha's back porch when she decided to call the police because we wouldn't give her any more money. When the police arrived, I should have taken a sign from everyone else who decided to scatter like roaches when you turn on the kitchen lights; but no, I decided I would attempt to finesse the police and talk to them. Although I felt I did nothing wrong at the time and I had no drugs on me, that decision led me to the back seat of a police car, which led me to the county jail for booking and fingerprinting and ultimately solitary confinement.

There I was, in a jail cell isolated from everyone and everything that I knew, and all I had was a Bible that I would begin to read. Before being locked in that cage, I don't recall a time in my life that I actually sat down to read the Bible. I had been to church, and I prayed off and on throughout my life, but it wasn't until then that I decided I needed a relationship with my Heavenly Father. So I began reading it earnestly. I came upon the book of Job, and as I read through the pages, I began to feel the richness of the Lord. A feeling of peace, belonging, and love began to overcome me. I also started to see a better vision for my life. The military came back to the forefront of my mind, and after much prayer and seeking guidance from the Lord, I made it my mission to never go back to the block unless I was doing some kingdom business; I also vowed to become twice the man I was prior to jail, like Job.

Chapter 3

VICTOR OR VICTIM

In life, I believe one comes to a point when they will have to decide to either be a victim or a victor of their circumstances. For me, that moment came when I found myself in solitary confinement, in a cell with no other human contact other than the guards coming to take me out for an hour so that I could walk around and shower or sliding me food through the door like a dog. I found out then that I couldn't get the victory alone and that I needed to create a lifelong bond with the Lord. After making that conscious decision, I began to get a glimpse of what could be my rich life. I was locked down for twenty-three hours a day with nothing but a metal toilet, a slab of concrete for my bed, a red blanket, and a Bible. It was in that cell where I began making Bible study a part of my life, searching the pages for some sign of hope, and kept coming back to the book of Job.

Job was a successful, loyal, faithful man and a servant of the Lord who had lost everything through no fault of his own. But despite losing all of what the world would consider riches and even his health, Job continued to give praise to and bless the Lord. And as I sat on that cold concrete slab wrapped in a thin red blanket, wiping tears of disappointment, confusion, and anger from my eyes, I began to reflect upon my own situation. Though I caused the storm I was currently in, I still couldn't understand how I was the first in my family to graduate high school, was the first to get accepted into college on a first-generation scholarship, and was supposed to be the chain breaker but was now locked up in a cell, far removed from the University of South Florida where I was attending classes a few months back.

I wasn't as wealthy as Job was before he was attacked by Satan with the Lord's permission, but I was on my way to breaking those chains that shackled my family for generations—chains of self-inflicted pain, poverty, drug abuse, prison, and family abandonment. Instead, I found myself in the same trap and not raising the bar as I intended to do when I was fresh out of high school. This realization was very humbling, and it was during this time of isolation that my relationship with the Lord began to deepen as I continued reading through the pages of the Bible, meditating on the words, and praying for what seemed like all day every day.

What was more revealing was the fact that I had been in jail for a couple of days and no one came to bond me out, see me, or anything. And soon I started to feel betrayed by those I trusted most. After a while though, I began to see man for who we are, truly connect with the Lord, and elevate my thoughts and feelings over my current circumstances. I was entering the richness of a relationship with the Lord, and that began to change my perspective of everything. From one of hopelessness to one of necessity. From one of a prisoner to one of a liberator. And as the days and hours passed, I began to realize it was necessary for the Lord to pull me from everyone and everything I thought I knew so that I could experience his rich peace, love, mercy, and grace.

Chapter 4

FAMILY MATTERS

After about ten days in solitary confinement, I was sober, stronger, and more determined than ever to live my rich life. I would wake up, say a prayer, and meditate before I began reading the Bible. It was also around this time that I found myself reading the gospel of Jesus. Here I was a sinner in my own right, flawed and lost in my ways, but God thought I was worthy enough to receive his love and forgiveness that he sent his only begotten Son to amend my sins.

As I read through the pages and witnessed miracle after miracle Jesus performed in the name of the Lord, I found myself becoming a fan. Simultaneously, my focus shifted entirely from being in jail to the wonders of Christ, on Almighty God and wanting to have my heart, mind, and soul renewed so that I too could become a beacon of light. I relished in the fact that God had forgiven me of my sins through the blood of Jesus, but somehow I still couldn't forgive myself or those who I felt had done me wrong. That was until I read and put into practice Matthew 6:14–15: "For if you forgive others their trespasses, your heavenly Father will also forgive you but if you do not forgive others their trespasses, neither will your Father forgive your trespasses." It was then I realized I harbored years of unforgiveness. I hadn't forgiven my father for deeming me unworthy to be his son and leaving me behind. I also hadn't forgiven my mother for all the years of physical and verbal abuse, but I realized I had to forgive them—not for them but for my own growth and spirituality and to also receive the fullness of my Heavenly Father. From day 10 to day 14, I would conduct an internal inventory and seek guidance from the Lord through Bible scriptures and meditation. Afterward, I felt equipped with the whole armor of God, and I felt ready for battle.

Chapter 5

MY RESURRECTION

The next day, Sheriff Jack came into my cell and said, "You're being released." Praise God! Throughout my time in solitary confinement, I was also doing push-ups, sit-ups, and jumping jacks for cardio, with hopes of following through on plans of joining the military. It was time to put the vision I received into action. I was released from jail a much richer man than I was before I truly encountered the Lord. Before, I was experiencing mental conflict between who I was, who I wanted to be, and who everyone else expected me to be. Now I was rich in peace, starting with a new life in the Lord. Before, I was also angry, angry at the condition of my people and my family and for not having the best in life. Now I was rich in joy, finding great pleasure and contentment in the small things in life that I did have. Before, I was lost, like a leaf blown in the wind after every man-made way of living. Now I was rich in purpose, having a clear understanding of not only who I was but whose I was and what I needed to do. And before I went to jail and connected with the Lord, I was dead, spiritually dead, merely going through the motions of life. Now I had a passion for living and a rich example of what one could do in Jesus Christ. I left jail determined to grow in this rich life and experience more of the Lord.

But as Luke 12:48 states, "But the one who did not know, and did what deserved a beating, will receive a light beating. Everyone to whom much was given, of him much will be required, and from him to whom they entrusted much, they will demand the more." And now I had my rich life in the Lord; I understood this rich life required higher standards, and I thought I had what was needed to live by those standards. But once I was physically freed from jail, I found myself questioning again: *Do you have what it takes to really live out this rich life?*

Chapter 6

MY RICH LIFE

S o there I was, a new man born again through the blood of Christ Jesus, now living in the free world, with nothing but high hopes and ambition burning off the top of my head in anticipation of growing in my rich life. That was until I moved back into my mother's house and became confronted with the same issues that tripped me up initially. It was easy to say what I would and wouldn't do when I wasn't in an environment that condoned such behavior, but by the grace of God, I realized early that how I responded when tempted would ultimately lead to my destination; and I wanted my rich life. So after I stayed with my family for a few days, I decided I wasn't going back to the block, so instead I went to reconnect with my girlfriend Charmaine, whom I hadn't seen for weeks.

Before the whole ordeal that led to me going to jail, it was just her and me, confiding in one another and pushing each other to be better since high school. Looking back, for the life of me, I never understood why I left her side. And I promised myself if she let me back in, I would never make the same mistake.

So I made my way over, and once I got to her mother's house, where she was living, I received the shock of my life. She was three months pregnant with my child!

Now I was only two days removed from solitary confinement, broke, unemployed, currently living with my mother, and soon to be a father. The pressure was mounting, and my situation looked nothing like the rich life I had envisioned. With all this added tension and new responsibilities, I had to go back into isolation with the Lord in prayer. Shortly after, I felt compelled to get deeper into the faith so that I could become the type of man who was capable of leading a family. After Charmaine and I reconciled our relationship and I explained to her the reason I disappeared and everything I had been through, it was time to keep pushing for my rich life.

First, I decided to go down to the local church and get baptized. Charmaine wanted to join me, but I felt it was best if I walked down this road alone so that I was sure I was doing this from a pure heart.

After that, I went down to the Air Force recruiter to enlist. But due to my recent jail time, I was barred from serving in the Air Force. I felt defeated, but I also felt a sense of calmness, like the Lord was telling me everything was going to be all right. So I went back to a practice I established in solitary confinement; I would wake up every day and connect with the Lord through prayer and Bible scriptures. During this time, I would also find work at the local temp agency while filling out job applications in anticipation of having my first child.

Throughout this period, I also began putting into practice the things that I learned added value to life while in solitary confinement. Along with meditation and reading Bible scriptures, I began to work out. And for six days a week, I would take twenty minutes for myself for Bible reading and meditation. I would also work out for another thirty minutes to an hour, doing more running than jumping jacks, and this became a practice I used to help shoulder the load I was under.

After about two months of this, I decided to go back to the recruiting station in hopes of serving in another branch of service, either the Army or the Marines, because there was no way I would become a seaman. This daily grind would soon pay dividends when I got a callback from the Army recruiter who asked me how would I like a twenty-thousand-dollar signing bonus for signing up to drive big trucks for the world's greatest army. My God! I couldn't contain my excitement. I was finally manifesting my rich life, and I knew that it was just the beginning!

Chapter 7

FATHERHOOD

I've come to realize that one of life's greatest riches is fatherhood. To be able to watch a life come into this world and have the opportunity to lead that life is priceless. I can recall throughout my childhood looking around the neighborhood and wondering, *We have all these mothers and kids, but where on earth are all the fathers?* I could never understand how someone could fix their lips to say they were a man knowing they had a child in this world that they created but were not breaking their neck to care for, not just in a monetary way but mentally, physically, and most importantly, spiritually. I grew up with the greatest disdain for the guy they said was my farther. It was so bad I can recall a period in my life that I had thoughts of harming him, but I thank God for growth.

My mother would have boyfriends throughout my childhood, but none cared enough to show me what it was to be a man. So in my early years and up into my teenage years, I would observe the things that men around me would do, men in the classroom and men from the block. I decided back then that if I ever had a child of my own, they would never have to doubt my love and commitment.

So now, I was a grown man, twenty years old, with my own child on the way—with nothing but the richness of a relationship with the Lord, a vision, my girlfriend, my mother, and hers. With that, I left home for basic training determined not to make the same tragic mistake my father made.

Chapter 8

MILITARY SERVICE

So there I was at Fort Sill, Oklahoma, in an all-male regiment—far from the block where I would see big cars riding on big rims. The only big wheels I saw were on tanks that would drive by our barracks from time to time. No friends. No family. Just me, a group of soon-to-be warriors, and a team of drill sergeants. The whole experience seems like a dream because I can only recall bits and pieces. I think I must have checked out mentally somewhere between arriving in a fifty-passenger cattle truck stuffed with 150 soldiers, the continuous smoke sessions from drill sergeants, and being screamed at from sunup to sundown. Throughout my time in basic training, I would find solace every Sunday when I would visit the chaplain and pray, and that became my weekly routine. We started basic training with 150 soldiers, but only a hundred made it to graduation. I believe I was part of that graduating class due to my relationship with the Lord and the rich power of prayer, which allowed me to endure and move forward when others couldn't.

After basic training, I attended AIT at Fort Leonard Wood, Oklahoma, and it was as if I was just released from a prison camp. The feeling of being a human was restored, and the instructors treated us like we were people instead of brainless robots. Throughout the duration of basic training and AIT, my girlfriend and I would correspond via handwritten letters, and our bond would be cemented. I can recall during my Bible study one evening reading Proverbs 18:22: "He who finds a wife finds a good thing and obtains favor from the LORD." I would meditate on those words for days as I thought of marriage and pondered the question, *Am I ready to be a husband?* I couldn't see myself as a husband just yet, though I knew who my wife was. So I decided I wouldn't propose to Charmaine and we would just raise our child together after I got home from AIT.

After training, again I was different—spiritually, physically, and mentally stronger than I had ever been prior to the experience and fully engulfed in the richness of the Lord. But when I got home, everything and everyone was the same; so again I found myself struggling to find my place, as I did after I was released from jail. After much prayer, scripture reading, and meditation, it became clearer that I wasn't meant to fit in. It was time for me to evolve and become the father I never had.

Chapter 9

TEST OF FAITH

After weeks of preparing for our son with the help of our parents, we were ready. On September 12, 2010, my son was born, and my perspective of myself and everyone else shifted further. It no longer mattered who thought I was cool and what they thought was cool. I now had a lifelong responsibility, and I was determined not to fail. The people I considered friends I had to keep at distance in order to become whom I envisioned—a God-fearing man who could lead a family, with strength and love. And making Charmaine my wife kept occurring in my thoughts, so after much prayer, I decided I would propose.

At the time, though I was mentally, physically, and spiritually rich, my situation had yet to reflect my current state. I was still living with my mother and doing odd jobs while serving as a private first class in the Army Reserve. So when I proposed to Charmaine the first time, I understood why she said no. I knew she was the wife the Bible spoke of because every time I prayed, I made sure I prayed for her as well.

I would go on struggling to create the rich life I envisioned for years, but I refused to quit because I felt rich within already; I just had to manifest it.

Carry and I would fight and make up every week during the first year of our son's life. I knew I had to do something to show her that I was the man she needed as much as she was the woman I needed. So I quit playing boyfriend and started being the husband she needed, even though she had yet to accept my proposal. After months of corrected behavior and showing Charmaine I was there for her and only her, I decided to propose again. She said yes!

Chapter 10

LIVING RICH

Carry and I would go on to have two more children: another boy and a baby girl. The richness I feel in being a father is worth more than any material possession. The richness I feel in being a husband and leader of a family only adds to my quality of living. I have become that hero and father that I wanted and felt I needed as a kid. I am also living the rich life I had envisioned while in solitary confinement.

I was deployed to Iraq and made it home safely, and I owe that to God because most of us didn't make it back. After I returned home, I went back to college and earned my bachelor's degree in business management. Simultaneously, I became a commissioned officer in the Army Reserve. Charmaine would go back to school as well and become a nurse. My mother and I have a growing relationship. Our family is prospering, strong, and healthy. And our kids have a relationship with the Lord.

I don't know what the future holds and what we will go through, but I do know that we will continue living the rich life—experiencing the abundant power, peace, love, and mercy of the Lord.

#Blessingz

About the Author

Sylvester L. Coston is a devoted husband and father of three beautiful children. A servant leader currently in the US Army, Sylvester has learned to put the needs of his family and team above his own, taking great pride in assisting others. Sylvester is on a mission to share his story and how his relationship with the Lord has provided him with an abundance of hope for the future and allowed him to convert past pains into power.

CPSIA information can be obtained
at www.ICGtesting.com
Printed in the USA
BVHW092041290322
632749BV00004B/674